101 THINGS

ABOUT TAYLOR SWIFT

First published in 2024 by Allsorted Ltd, WD19 4BG U.K.

The facts and statistics in this book are correct up to the end of 2022. Data comes from publicly available sources and is presented as correct as far as our knowledge allows. Any views or opinions represented in this book are personal and belong solely to the book author and are not intended to malign any religious community, ethnic group, club, organization, company or individual.

ISBN 9781915902740

Printed in Lithuania.

101 THINGS TO DO WHILE …

OBSESSING ABOUT TAYLOR SWIFT

ALLSORTED.
WD19 4BG U.K.

INTRODUCTION

In the whirlwind world of pop culture, few stars shine as brightly as Taylor Swift. Whether you're a die-hard Swiftie or just someone who can't get her catchy tunes out of your head, **101 Things to Do While Obsessing About Taylor Swift** is your ultimate companion. This book is packed with fun activities that offer a delightful break from your Taylor obsession, while still celebrating the magic she brings into your life

1.

FANTASY FESTIVAL LINEUP

Who is in your ultimate festival lineup and who would the headliner be?

You can feature artists from any era. Text the list to a friend and see if they approve

2.

HAIRSTYLE HALL OF FAME

Grab some paper and a pen and sketch out the most iconic hairdos from music history

3.

ICE-CREAM INNOVATION

Get creative in the kitchen and come up with a new ice-cream flavour by adding your favourite ingredients to a vanilla base

4.

TRUE OR FALSE?

1

Justin Bieber has a fear of pineapples

2

The Rihanna song "Umbrella" was originally offered to Britney Spears, but her label rejected it

3

Bruno Mars is actually the stage name of Frank Pluto

(A: 1. false, 2. true, 3. false)

5.

WEIRD RIDER

Have fun brainstorming the strangest diva-style demands you'd make backstage if you were a performer. Now try seeing if your friends or family will indulge you in your own living room

6.

DIGITAL DECLUTTERING

1.
Delete all the apps on your phone that you hardly ever use

2.
Now get rid of all the multiple versions of photos

Phew! That feels better

☑

7.

DESERT ISLAND MEAL

Imagine your perfect meal down to every last detail. Why not try making it – or learn to make it – and then invite your BFF to join you at the feast?

8.

THREE THANKS

Take a moment to reflect on the three things you're most grateful for in your life right now

1

2

3

9.

MAKING MOVES

Have some fun and invent a new dance move, complete with a catchy name. Next time you're with your friends, try it out and see if it sticks

10.

JUST TODAY

Find some paper and write a short poem about your thoughts and feelings in the last 24 hours

Thoughts & Feelings

11.

SWIFTIE CHARADES

Divide players into teams, with each team taking turns to act out Taylor Swift song titles while the other team members guess. Experiment with time limits, point systems and prizes to make it even more fun

12.

DIY MUSIC VIDEO

Film a music video on your phone for your all-time favourite song

13.

LAUGHTER THERAPY

Watch funny videos, tell jokes, or just think of something – real or imaginary – that you find hilarious. It's an instant mood boost and doesn't cost a penny

14.

SPRINKLE JOY LIKE CONFETTI

Perform random acts of kindness for others. You could leave an uplifting note, pay for someone's coffee, or offer a compliment to brighten someone's day

15.

TABLETOP TOURNAMENT

Gather your friends or family for a board-game marathon. Dust off your old favourites or try out new ones

16.

BFF LINGO

Develop some phrases in a completely new language that only you and your BFFs can understand

17.

PET JAM

Curate a playlist of songs that you think your pet would enjoy – then have a listening party with your animal pal

18.

NOSTALGIA BINGE

Rediscover old books, toys or games that you remember fondly from childhood – or get online and find photos and video clips of these comforting cultural creations

19.

CINEMA SURPRISE

Pack a movie-themed picnic basket and head to a nearby park or beach. Enjoy the fresh air, sunshine and good company while munching on delicious treats. Can your friends guess the film from the snacks?

20.

THE ULTIMATE GIG

Let your imagination run wild and sketch out your fantasy concert venue on paper from the comfort of your own home

21.

SENSORY SCAVENGER HUNT

Identify as many sounds as you can hear right now. How many have you counted?

22.

PODCAST PERFECTION

Decide on four guests for your dream podcast. What would you ask them?

23.

PILLOW FORT PARADISE

Build a pillow fort in your living room and escape into your own private sanctuary. Fill it with blankets, cushions and fairy lights

24.

FASHION FLOPS

Invite your BFFs over to strut their stuff on the runway (aka your living-room carpet) wearing their most cringeworthy outfits

25.

WHISTLE WHILE YOU WORK IT

CAN ANYONE TELL THE SONG?

IF NOT, TRY HUMMING IT INSTEAD!

26.

ONCE UPON AN EMOJI

Create a story about a day in the life of a pop star using only emojis and send it to someone to test if they can translate it back to you

27.

SONGWRITING SCOOP

Did you know that One Direction's "Little Things" was written by Ed Sheeran when he was only 17?

Jessie J wrote Miley Cyrus's hit "Party in the USA" and apparently it paid her rent for three years

Harry Styles was also a writer on Ariana Grande's song "Just a Little Bit of Your Heart"

28.

IN THE BAG

Can you list everything in your handbag or pockets without looking?

2 points for each correct item

29.

YOU'RE GORGEOUS!

Look in the mirror, give yourself a winning smile, and say three things you like about yourself

30.

SLIP 'N' SLIDE SOCK-SKATING

Put on a pair of socks and turn your smooth floor into an impromptu skating rink. Glide around the room, slide, twirl, and try not to slip as you enjoy some silly sock-skating fun

31.

RATE THESE QUEEN TAYLOR QUOTES

"Just be yourself, there is no one better."

"In life and love, you learn that there comes a time to let go and move on."

"I think fearless is having fears but jumping anyway."

32.

BEDROOM BLITZ

It's time for a total room revamp. Move the furniture around, change the posters and throw out any dead plants or useless junk

33.

SLUMBER PARTY

Invite your BFFs over for the perfect self-care slumber party. Must include: PJs, popcorn and pillow fights

34.

ROAD TRIP RUNDOWN

Search online for ideas and map out your dream road trip. Don't forget to list the snacks, playlist and pit stops and text it to the person you'd most like to go with

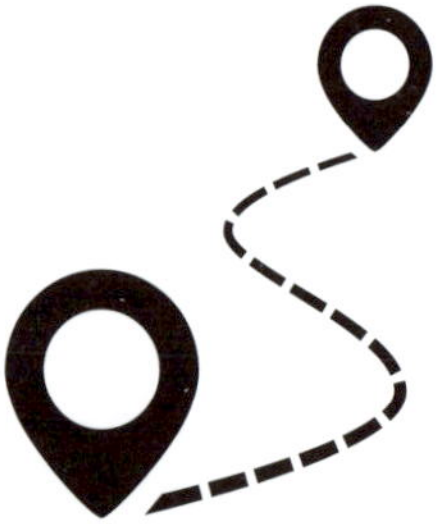

35.

RECONNECT WITH A TEXT

Send a "Hey there!" text to someone you haven't spoken to in forever

36.

STARRY DINNER PARTY

Which five celebrity guests would you invite? What's the seating arrangement and what's on the menu? Call a friend and see if they agree

37.

ANIMAL AURA

Ask your BFF what they think your spirit animal is and why – then do the same for your friend

38.

TOOTHPASTE TWIST

Carefully remove the filling from some Oreo cookies and replace it with toothpaste. Offer them to your sibling or BFF and watch – or even better, film – their reaction when they take a bite

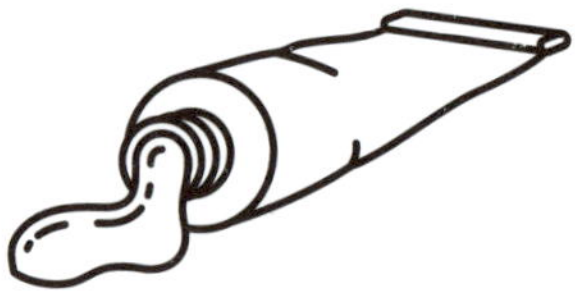

39.

ROCK & ROLL PAINTING

Find smooth rocks outside and paint them to resemble animals, emojis or your favourite fictional characters. Hide them around your neighbourhood for others to find

40.

SEVEN-YEAR SCHEME

Set goals for where you want to be in seven years and write them in a journal to look back on in the future

41.

SKY-HIGH SHOPPING

Look up at the sky and decide which cloud looks most like a designer dress, handbag or lipstick

42.

PUZZLED

Which five-letter word, when typed in all capitals, can be read the same upside down?

(Answer: SWIMS)

43.

EDIBLE EMOJIS

Use slices of fruit such as strawberries, oranges and kiwis to create a funny face on a plate. Get creative with expressions and hairstyles and offer it to a friend to see if it makes them smile

44.

YOU'RE A WINNER!

If you won a huge amount of money, how would you spend it – who would you treat and why?

45.

TIME CAPSULE CHALLENGE

Choose five items to represent this year so far – you could either note these down on paper and seal it in an envelope to be opened many years from now, or you could create an actual time capsule and bury it in your back yard

M

1. ....

2. ....

3. ....

4. ....

5. ....

46.

PAPER PALS

Learn to create origami animals like frogs, birds or butterflies. There are many tutorial videos online. You can use any type of paper – old magazines, newspapers, wrapping paper – to recycle and transform it into something beautiful

47.

LOOK AROUND YOU AND HUNT FOR...

3 things that are red

2 things that are green

1 thing that is yellow

48.

LIT LOVE BOOK CLUB

Plan what you're going to get everyone to read first, then invite your friends over for some bookish banter. Don't forget to offer perfectly themed snacks

49.

SERENADE YOUR PET

Sing a silly song to your animal companion. You must use the following words from Taylor Swift's songs: matinee, dynasty and Sunday

50.

YES DAY

Offer your friend a "yes" day where you will spend a day doing whatever they want (within reason!) and see if they'll do the same for you

51.

DIY ESCAPE ROOM

Gather your friends and split into two teams. Each team must transform a room into an interactive puzzle adventure: create clues, riddles and challenges that lead to the ultimate goal of "escaping" the room within a set time limit, then put the other team to the test

52.

APP ATTACK

Invent an app that should exist but doesn't. What does it do? How does it work?

Pitch it to a friend and see if they love your innovative tech idea

53.

ITALIAN INKLING

Learn these Italian words:

- Ciao (Hi)
- Grazie (Thank you)
- Sĩ (Yes)
- No (No)
- Arrivederci (Goodbye)
- Per favore (Please)
- Certo (Sure)

54.

LIPSTICK LIST

How many lipstick colours can you name?

Try imagining a completely new colour with a made-up name

55.

JUKEBOX JOURNEY

Create a playlist of songs that remind you of significant moments in your life, from childhood memories to recent adventures. Press play and reminisce about the good times

56.

THROW YOUR OWN FILM FESTIVAL

Curate a movie marathon that reflects your cinematic tastes. Now get comfy and start watching. Don't forget the snacks and the standing ovations

57.

ME MUSEUM

What six items would be in a museum exhibit about you?

Collect them up and make a mini display

58.

VIRTUAL VENUE

Host a concert party where you play live performances or live recordings from favourite artists. Set up a projector or large screen, dim the lights and enjoy it like you're there in person

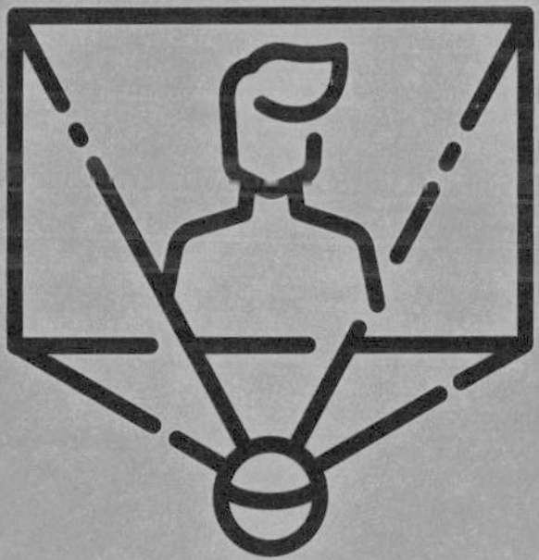

59.

HOMEMADE HARMONIES

Get crafty and make your own DIY musical instruments using household items. You could make shakers with rice and empty containers, drums with pots and pans, or guitars with rubber bands and cardboard boxes. Then jam out with your friends or write a song together

60.

LIFE LAUGHS

Pitch the pilot episode of a new TV sitcom based on your own life to someone in your family and see what they think

61.

COSMIC BEATS

If you were going to space, what songs would you listen to on the voyage?

Create a playlist that's out of this world

62.

ENVISION YOUR PARADISE

Forget Pinterest and go old school. Gather magazines, scissors, glue and a large piece of paper. Cut out images and words that represent your goals and aspirations, then arrange them on your board to create a visual representation of your dreams

63.

CREATIVE QUEST

Challenge yourself to do something creative every day for a week. Share your creations on social media to inspire others

64.

MOOD MIXOLOGY

Select the ingredients from your fridge and cupboards for a cocktail or mocktail that captures your essence – taste it and name it

65.

LAUGH IT UP

Draw the silliest picture you can imagine on a scrap of paper, then show it to a friend to make them giggle

66.

TEXTURE TREK

Look around your room or go outside and find:

3 things that are soft

2 things that are rough

1 thing that is smooth

67.

SECRET SHAKE

Invent a unique, elaborate handshake that only you and your BFF can perform

68.

INVENT AN AWARDS SHOW

What's the name of the show? What awards would you give out? Best-dressed pet? Most creative late night snack?

Text the winners with the news of their new awards

69.

STAR STYLE SPY

Look around you. Can you match four people who are near you right now with their celebrity lookalikes?

70.

MINDFUL MUNCHIES

Really savour each bite of your next treat, noticing its fragrance, texture and flavour

71.

SOLO SHIMMY

Let go of your inhibitions and dance like nobody is watching. You could even switch the lights off if it helps!

72.

WARDROBE REVOLUTION

Host a fashion swap party with friends to exchange old items of clothing from your wardrobe

73.

SELFIE SOIRÉE

GO TO YOUR FAVOURITE PLACE FOR A BITE TO EAT AND TREAT YOURSELF TO SOME ALONE TIME TO INDULGE AND REFLECT. YOU REALLY DO DESERVE IT

M

74.

SOUNDS AWFUL

Create a terrible playlist of horrendous songs that would be perfect for your worst enemy or an evil ex

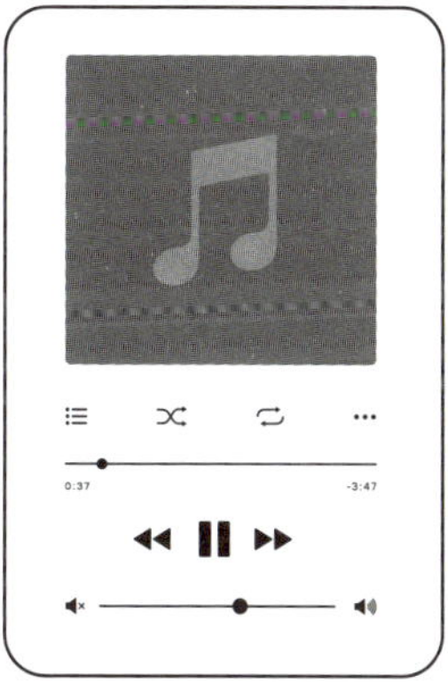

75.

START A FLASH MOB

Instigate your own flash mob performance in a public place, even if it's just you dancing to music you're hearing through your headphones

76.

FASHION SHOOT

Organize a photoshoot with friends where you all model your favourite outfits

77.

VINTAGE SHOP CRAWL

Search through vintage or thrift shops with your friends – set a budget and see who can find the best or most hilarious outfit

78.

BRAIN BENDERS

What goes up but never comes down?

What has buttons but can't be pushed?

What can you wear that never goes out of style?

(Answer: age, shirt, smile)

79.

SWIFTIE SONG COVER CHALLENGE

Challenge your friends to perform their own covers of Taylor Swift songs, either by singing or playing instruments

80.

PIXEL PARTY

Grab your smartphone and embark on a photography adventure. Explore different genres such as portrait photography, street photography and macro photography

81.

MOTIVATIONAL MOTTO

Come up with a unique mantra, stick it up somewhere you will see it, and repeat it to yourself every day

82.

MOVIE MODE

Plan and host a fashion-themed movie marathon. Be sure to dress for the occasion

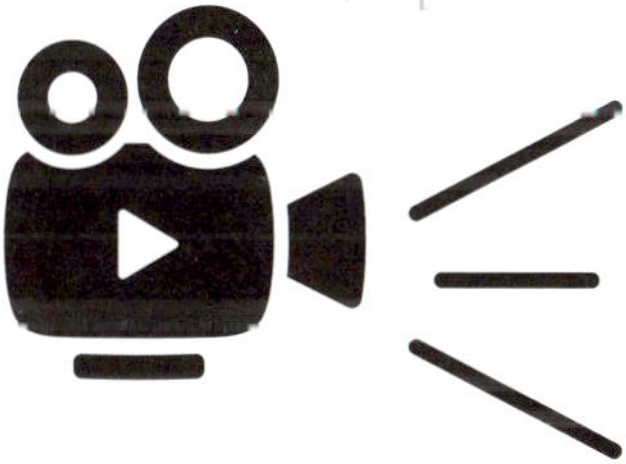

83.

STARRY SKIES

Head outside on a clear night and do some stargazing. Lay out a blanket and marvel at the beauty of the night sky while identifying constellations and shooting stars

M

84.

LOVE LETTER

Write a love note to yourself – what are your most adorable qualities? Put it somewhere safe and reread it in a year's time

85.

KITCHEN CREATIVITY

Come up with a unique recipe for a delicious dish. If you're feeling confident, try it out – you might just invent a new classic

WELL DONE!

86.

GOOD DEEDS DASH

Plan five kind acts to do this week and give yourself a little treat every time you complete one

1. ....

2. ....

3. ....

4. ....

5. ....

87.

SCREEN SLAY

Say goodbye to screens and hello to real-life adventures for 24 hours as you rediscover the joy of being offline. How will you spend your free time instead?

88.

BUBBLE BLISS

Treat yourself to the perfect bubble bath – complete with bath bombs, scented candles and soothing music – to help you relax and recharge

89.

MINDFUL LISTENING

Give the next person
who talks to you
your full attention
without interrupting
or thinking about
what you'll say next

90.

GUESS THE THEME TUNE

Hum a popular theme tune or song from a movie or TV show – and get others to guess what it is. It's a fun way to test each other's knowledge and reminisce about favourite films and series

✓

91.

HEY SHORTY

Today 10:00

Challenge yourself to tell a story

using only six words

and text it to your BFF to see what they think

Read

....

92.

PICK YOUR FAVOURITE FEEL-GOOD QUOTE

"Find out who you are
and do it on purpose."
– Dolly Parton

"Friends are the
family we choose."
– Jennifer Aniston

"Try to be a rainbow in
someone else's cloud."
– Maya Angelou

93.

EMOTION CHECK-IN

Reflect on your current feelings and identify:

3 things
that make you
feel happy

2 things
that make you
feel calm

1 thing
that makes you
feel excited

94.

UNLEASH THE TALENT

Host a talent show where your friends showcase their hidden talents, whether it's singing, dancing, magic tricks or stand-up comedy

95.

CANDLE CREATION

Get together with friends to make your own DIY candles using wax, wicks and essential oils. Experiment with different scents and colours to create personalized candles that reflect your unique tastes

96.

DECADE DISCO

How about a Seventies disco night or a roaring Twenties soirée? Plan a time-travelling playlist, put together an eye-catching outfit, make period-perfect snacks – it's up to you!

97.

FORTUNE FORECAST

Have fun with friends by trying out different fortune-telling methods like tarot cards, palm reading or tea-leaf reading. See what insights or laughs you can gain from the experience

98.

ME MOMENT

Plan a unique daily routine that includes meditation, journaling, exercise and relaxation – and try to do it every day

99.

NAIL NOTES

Create nail art designs inspired by your favourite songs – or maybe celebrate a whole album across both hands

100.

DID YOU KNOW?

Ed Sheeran has more than 60 tattoos covering his body

Billie Eilish's full name is Billie Eilish Pirate Baird O'Connell

The name of K-Pop group BTS translates as "Bulletproof Boy Scouts"

101.

GRATITUDE GALORE

Grab an empty jar and fill it with jotted-down blessings on pieces of paper, giving thanks for the awesomeness in your life. Open up the jar and pick out a piece of positivity whenever you need a boost